The empanada COOKBOOK

Easy and Tasty Empanada Recipes!

THE EMPANADA COOKBOOK

MAKING EMPANADAS IS FUN WITH THESE MOUTH-WATERING AND TASTY RECIPES

By
Savour Press
Copyright © by Wentworth Publishing House
All rights reserved

Published by
Savour Press, a DBA of Wentworth Publishing House

Let's get it started!

Welcome to Savour. Just as so many, we live for the joy that food or even cooking brings. Whether you're brushing up on how to give your hand-cut fries the crispiness of a potato chip or getting your keto, veganism diet on (and seriously, who's not these days?), look no further. In our philosophy, cooking is not meant to be dreadful, or to take up your entire day, or contain a ton of stuff you have that has you running to that hipster grocery store for (you know who you are). It's meant to be delicious, fun and dare we say savory? overall, it's supposed to be a fun and exciting time. We don't just want to collect dust we want a place on your kitchen top as you fry, bake or boil. That's why we filled this book with an all-star collection of recipes so that you can confidently put on the cooking hat whenever the urge strikes you!

Also, by the editors at Savour Press's kitchen

The Chili Cookbook

The Quiche Cookbook

Indian Instant Pot Cookbook

The Cajun and Creole Cookbook

The Grill Cookbook

The Burger Book

The Ultimate Appetizers Cookbook

The West African Cookbook

Korean Seoul Cookbook

About This Book

So often we ask ourselves "if only I could have this at home, I want to know how to make this?" Well, that's where Savour comes in.

Savour This is just that. It opens with a recipe of cheese empanadas that is delicious for all people. All the recipes included in this book are not only delicious but they are super fun to make. We guarantee that you and your family would definitely enjoy creating delicious and healthy empanada recipes. Let's get ready to have a fun time!

Copyright © 2018 by Savour Press

All rights reserved. No part of this publication may be reproduced, distributed, or transmitted in any form or by any means, including photocopying, recording, or other electronic or mechanical methods, without the prior written permission of the publisher, except in the case of brief quotations embodied in critical reviews and certain other noncommercial uses permitted by copyright law.

Table of Contents

Introduction pg 10

Cheese Empandas pg 12

Jalapeno Popper Chicken Empanadas pg 13

Pineapple Empanadas pg 15

Spinach & Cheese Empanadas pg 18

Pork Empanadas pg 21

Chorizo & Cheese Empanadas pg 23

Chocolate & Banana Empanadas pg 25

Mini-Beef Empanadas pg 27

Sweet Corn Red Pepper & Green Chili Empanadas pg 29

Peach Empanadas pg 30

Chicken Enchilada Empanadas pg 32

Caramel Apple Empanadas pg 33

Shephard's Pie Empanadas pg 35

Chocolate Dulce de leche Empanadas pg 37

Black Bean Empanadas pg 39

Chicken & Mushroom Empanadas pg 40

S'mores Empanadas pg 43

Berry & Ricotta Empanadas pg 44

Roasted Veggie Empanadas pg 46

Breakfast Empanadas pg 48

Colombian Empanadas pg. 50

Strawberry Empanadas pg 52

Mushroom & Cheese Empanadas pg 54

Raisin & Arroz con leche Empanadas pg 55

Argentinian Beef Empanadas pg 57

Conclusion pg 60

Introduction

"If you were a Colombian, you would have your version of an empanada. If you are an Argentinean, you might find a dough that's baked and has a butter sheen on it. And then in Ecuador, you'll find more crispy-fried empanadas. So, yeah, every culture has their own version of empanadas."

Jose Garces

Jose Garces has pretty much summed up the importance of empanadas in a great way. Yes, the empanadas really are a part of every culture but every culture has its own version of empanadas. It is baked in some areas and some cultures prefer fried empanadas. Some people like sweet empanadas whereas, others love a bit sour touch in their empanadas. Basically, empanada comes from a Portuguese word "empanar" which means "to wrap something in a bread". It doesn't matter what your preference is, you will always find an empanada recipe suitable for your taste buds. If you are just getting started or you love making delicious recipes for your friends, this book has got you covered. You will find many delicious empanada recipes that you can easily make at your home.

Cheese Empanadas

Here is the first recipe of empanadas – Cheese Empanadas. This recipe is one of the easiest recipes that you can make in no time. You can also freeze the leftover dough to use later.

Ingredients

5 cups flour

grated mozzarella 4 cups

1 tsp salt

A bowl warm water

200 Ml from a package of lard

Directions

Add flour, lard, and salt to a bowl and mix properly.

Add 2 cups warm water to the flour mixture and knead the dough.

Roll a small section of dough and form round empanadas with the help of a cookie cutter.

Take 1 tbsp. mozerella and fill it in the empanadas. Fold it and seal with a finger. Use a fork to firmly press the edges.

Heat the oil in a large skillet and fry the empanadas until brown.

Once done, remove from the skillet and serve.

Enjoy!

Nutritional Information: 162 Cal, 18 g Fat, 40 mg Chol, 330 mg Sodium, 8 g Protein.

Jalapeno Popper Chicken Empanadas

These jalapeno popper chicken empanadas are all you need on a boring Monday night. They are made with shredded chicken, corn, cheese, and jalapenos.

Ingredients

Pastry:

4 cups all-purpose flour

¾ cups cold unsalted butter

1 tablespoon coarse salt

2 teaspoons baking powder

1 + ¼ cups ice water

Filling:

8 ounces full fat cream cheese

⅓ cup sour cream

1 + ½ cups fresh shredded cheddar cheese

½ cup corn

2 cups cooked shredded chicken

1 tablespoon milk or water

1 beaten egg

4 ounce can diced jalapenos

salt and black pepper, to taste

Directions

Mix all the ingredients of pastry in a bowl and mix properly. Knead to form a soft dough.

Divide the dough into small sections and refrigerate for 1 hour.

Melt cream cheese in a bowl and add shredded chicken to it.

Add all the remaining ingredients except egg and milk to it. Mix well.

Take a separate bowl and add milk and egg to it and beat.

Roll the small sections of refrigerated dough on a floured surface.

Cut the dough into small pieces using a cookie cutter.

Take 1 tbsp. of cream cheese mixture and place it onto the empanadas. Do it with all the dough pieces.

Using your finger, paint the corners of empanadas with water and fold. Press the edges.

Grease a baking sheet and preheat your oven to 400 F.

Use a pastry brush to brush empanadas with the egg mixture.

Bake for about 18 minutes.

Serve and enjoy!

Nutritional Information: 710 Cal, 56.7 g Fat, 175 mg Chol, 1159 mg Sodium, 31 g Protein.

Pineapple Empanadas

These sweet pineapple empanadas are made with delicious homemade filling. Their sweet taste is quite unique. Your family will surely fall in love with it!

Ingredients

For the Dough

3½ cups flour

1¼ cups shortening

1/2 cup sugar

1 teaspoon baking powder

another 1/2 cup sugar for dusting empanadas

1/2 teaspoon anise seeds

1- branch cinnamon stick

1 teaspoon salt

2 tablespoons cinnamon ground

1/2 cup water

For the pineapple filling

3/4 cup dark brown sugar

1½ tablespoons cornstarch

2 cups pineapple finely chopped

1/4 cup cold water

2 tablespoons lemon juice

Directions

Take a bowl and add anise seeds, ½ cup water and cinnamon stick to it. Microwave for 1 minute.

Add shortening to the cinnamon mixture and mix properly.

Take a separate bowl and mix all the dry ingredients of dough in it.

Mix the dry and wet ingredients together. Cover it and set aside.

To make the pineapple filling, heat the pineapple in a skillet.

Add brown sugar and lemon juice to the skillet. Cook for about 25 minutes.

Take a separate bowl and mix ¼ cup cold water and cornstarch in it. Add it to the pineapple mixture and cook for another 5 minutes.

Now it is time to make empanadas. Preheat your oven to 375 F. Divide dough into small balls and roll it.

Place 1 to 2 tbsp of filling in each empanada circle.

Fold the empanadas and seal properly. Press the edges.

Place empanadas over a baking sheet and bake for about 25 minutes.

Dust cinnamon and sugar over empanadas.

Serve!

Nutritional Information: 68 Cal, 2 g Fat, 12 mg Chol, 83 mg Sodium, 1 g Protein.

Spinach & Cheese Empanadas

If you want to try something different today, then try to make these super delicious spinach and cheese empanadas.

Ingredients

Empanada dough

1 cup water
2 3/4 cups flour
2 tsp salt

3/4 cup lard
pinch paprika

Spinach cheese filling

2 tbsps olive oil

1 tbsp butter
1 tsp chile powder

3 cloves garlic, minced
5-8 oz fresh spinach
8 oz whole milk mozzarella cheese, shredded

1 cup ricotta cheese

salt and pepper to taste

2 tbsps Parmesan cheese, grated

Directions

To make the dough, mix all the dough ingredients together and knead well. Cover with a plastic wrap and set aside.

Heat oil in a skillet and add chili powder and minced garlic to it. Cook for one minute.

Add spinach, to the skillet and cook again for about 7 minutes.

Once done, remove from the heat and add mozzarella cheese, ricotta cheese, parmesan cheese to it. Season with salt and pepper.

Preheat your oven to 375 F.

Roll the dough and make small circles using a cookie cutter.

Place 1-2 tbsp of spinach filling on each circle and seal the empanadas by pressing the edges.

Place empanadas on a baking sheet and bake for about 25 minutes.

Serve and enjoy!

Nutritional Information: 28 Cal, 16 g Fat, 105 mg Chol, 612 mg Sodium.

Pork Empanada

These empanadas are filled with pork and served with a dip or salsa. It can serve as a great appetizer as well as a snack.

Ingredients

Filling

1 tbsp olive oil 15 mL

1/2 jalapeño pepper, chopped 1/2

1 tbsp minced garlic 15 mL

1/2 yellow onion, chopped 1/2

1 tsp ground cumin 5 mL

1 tsp smoked paprika 5 mL

1 lb ground pork 500 g

1 tsp ground coriander 5 mL

1/4 cup chopped fresh cilantro 60 mL

1/4 cup chopped green olives 60 mL

Salt and freshly ground black pepper

1/3 cup golden raisins 75 mL

Salsa Verde

1/2 cup chopped white onion 125 mL

2 tsp minced garlic 10 mL

2 cups chopped tomatillos 500 mL

1 serrano chile pepper, seeded and minced 1

1/4 cup chopped fresh cilantro leaves 60 mL

1/2 tsp salt 2 mL

2 recipes All-Butter Pie Dough

2 tbsp freshly squeezed lime juice 30 mL

1 large egg, lightly beaten with 1 tbsp water

Canola or safflower oil

Directions

Heat oil in a skillet. Add jalapeno, onion, garlic, paprika, cumin and coriander to it. Saute for about 5 minutes.

Add pork to the skillet and saute again for about 5 minutes.

Add cilantro, olives and raisins to the skillet and mix well. Season with salt and pepper. Set aside.

To make salsa verde, add all the ingredients in a blender and blend until a paste is formed.

Transfer this mixture to a pan and cook on medium heat for 5 minutes. Once done, remove from the heat and set aside.

Roll the dough and cut into small circles by using a cookie cutter.

Brush the dough circles with egg wash.

Place 1-2 tbsp of filling on each circle and fold the empanadas. Press the edges and seal properly.

Place the empanadas on a baking sheet and freeze for 1 hour.

After 1 hour, remove the empanadas from the freezer and bake for 20 minutes.

Serve warm!

Nutritional Information: 395 Cal, 22.4 g Fat, 68 mg Chol, 686 mg Sodium, 21 g Protein.

Chorizo & Cheese Empanadas

Here is an easy and mouthwatering recipe of chorizo and cheese empanadas. If you like fried empanadas, you can fry these as well.

Ingredients

Empanada dough 2 cups

Choriqueso filling:

1 tablespoon butter or olive oil

1 lb. Mexican style fresh chorizo

½ white onion, finely diced – about 1 cup

3 cups or 12 ounces of grated mozzarella

½ to 1 tablespoon of ground achiote

1 cup or 4 ounces of crumbled queso fresco,

If baking:

1 egg yolk + 1 tablespoon water

Directions

Heat the oil in a skillet and add onion to it. Cook for about 5 minutes.

Break the chorizo into chunks. Add it to the skillet and cook on medium heat until the meat is fully cooked.

Mix queso fresco and mozzarella in a bowl.

Roll the empanada dough and cut into small circles by using a cookie cutter.

Place 1-2 tbsp of chorizo and cheese mix on each circle and fold the empanadas. Press the edges and seal properly.

Place the empanadas on a baking sheet and freeze for 1 hour.

After 1 hour, remove the empanadas from the freezer.

Brush with egg wash and bake on 400 F for 20 minutes.

Serve warm!

Nutritional Information: 290 Cal, 11.5 g Fat, 57 mg Chol, 665 mg Sodium, 11 g Protein.

Chocolate & Banana Empanadas

Craving for something sweet? Use this recipe to make incredibly delicious chocolate and banana empanadas. They are delicious, sweet and healthy at the same time.

Ingredients

1 cup Empanada Dough

4 ounces bittersweet chocolate

1/2cup butter

2tablespoons sugar

6tablespoons cake flour

2egg yolks

2tablespoons chopped peanuts

1/2of a medium banana, finely chopped

2teaspoons rum

2teaspoons powdered sugar

1egg

1tablespoon water

Directions

Melt chocolate and butter in a bowl and add sugar to it.

Add flour to the chocolate mixture and mix well. Now add egg yolks, rum and banana to this mixture and stir well. Set aside for 30 minutes.

Preheat oven to 425 F and grease the baking sheet.

Make empanadas by using empanada dough and chocolate filling.

Transfer the empanadas to the baking sheet and bake for 15 minutes or until the empanadas become brown.

Once done, remove from the oven and let them cool.

Dust with sugar and serve!

Nutritional Information: 198 Cal, 24 g Fat, 34 mg Chol, 81 mg Sodium, 3 g Protein.

Mini Beef Empanadillas

Mini beef empanadillas are great for holiday season because you can make this recipe in no time. They are also known as beef turnovers. These empanadillas are just like empanadas but the dough will be a bit thinner in this recipe.

Ingredients

Dough-
2 cups all-purpose white flour
1 teaspoon salt
1 stick of butter (cold)
1 egg
3/4 or a cup of cold water

Beef Filling-
2 lbs of ground beef
Adobo (or salt & pepper)
1/4 cup of Sofrito
1 small envelope of Sazon
2 garlic cloves (peeled and chopped)
1/2 of an onion diced
1/2 green pepper diced
1/2 red pepper diced
1 small potato diced
1 cup of tomato sauce

Directions

Mix all the dough ingredients in a food processor. Add water until the mixture becomes stretchy.

Cover the dough and refrigerate for about 1 hour.

To make the beef filling, add ground beef, adobo, and garlic cloves in a skillet and cook until the meat becomes brown.

Add tomato sauce, sazon, onions, sofrito, green peppers, potatoes and red peppers to the skillet and cook for another 15 minutes.

Roll the empanada dough and cut into small circles by using a cookie cutter.

Place 1 tbsp of beef filling on each empanadilla and seat tightly using a fork.

Deep fry the empanadillas in oil until they become brown.

Serve and enjoy!

Nutritional Information: 200 Cal, 5 g Fat, 10 mg Chol, 470 mg Sodium, 8 g Protein.

Sweet Corn, Red Pepper & Green Chile Empanadas

Sweet corn, red pepper and green chili empanadas are stuffed with nutritious veggies and its recipe is quite simple as well.

Ingredients

2 tablespoons butter

½ white onion, finely diced

3 cloves garlic, minced

1 red bell pepper, finely diced

1 (12 ounce) frozen corn

1 can green chiles diced

1 tablespoons fresh oregano

1 pinch salt and ground pepper

1 can Refrigerated Biscuits

Directions

Preheat oven to 350 F.

Take a medium-sized pan and melt butter in it. Add garlic and onion to the pan and saute for about 3 minutes.

Add oregano, red pepper, green chilies, a pinch of salt and pepper, and corn to the pan. Cook for another 5 minutes.

Roll the empanada dough and cut into small circles by using a cookie cutter.

Place 2 tbsp of veggie mixture on the empanada circles. Seal properly using a fork.

Place the empanadas on a non-greased baking sheet and bake for 15 minutes.

Serve immediately!

Nutritional Information: 230 Cal, 13 g Fat, 15 mg Chol, 470 mg Sodium, 6 g Protein.

Peach Empanadas

If you have some peaches in your fridge then the best thing that you can do with them is making peach empanadas. Use the following recipe to make delicious empanadas stuffed with peaches.

Ingredients

Fresh peach filling:

8 cups peeled and diced peaches

1 cup sugar

1/2 cup water

2 cinnamon sticks

3 whole cloves

Empanada dough:

3 cups all-purpose flour

2 teaspoons baking powder

½ teaspoon salt

½ cup shortening

2 eggs

½ cup milk

2 tablespoons granulated sugar

Directions

Add peaches, water, sugar, and cloves to a pan and bring to a boil. Cook until the peaches become soft.

Discard cinnamon, excess water and cloves. Cook for another 15 minutes.

To make the empanada dough. Mix all the dough ingredients and knead properly.

Cover the dough with a plastic wrap and refrigerate for 30 minutes.

After 30 minutes, roll the empanada dough and cut into small circles by using a cookie cutter.

Place 1 tbsp of peach filling on each circle and seal properly by pressing the edges.

Brush the empanadas with egg wash and sprinkle some cinnamon over them.

Spray a baking sheet with cooking spray and place empanadas over this baking sheet.

Bake in a preheated oven for about 20 minutes.

Serve and enjoy!

Nutritional Information: 51 Cal, 0.3 g Fat, 0 mg Chol, 0 mg Sodium, 1.2 g Protein.

Chicken Enchilada Empanadas

This chicken enchilada empanadas recipe is a mixture of delicious empanadas and enchiladas. It can be served as an appetizer as well as a snack.

Ingredients

2 sheets puff pastry, thawed

2 cups shredded chicken

½ cup enchilada sauce

1 cup shredded Mexican blend cheese

1 egg + 1 tablespoon water mixed together in small bowl

Sour cream, green onion, cilantro for garnish

Directions

Preheat your oven to 375 F.

Mix enchilada sauce and chicken in a medium-sized bowl.

Roll the pastry sheet in divide into small circles.

Place 2 tbsp chicken mixture over pasty circles and sprinkle with cheese. Seal tightly.

Poke two holes on each empanada and brush with eggs. Sprinkle some cheese over them.

Bake for about 25 minutes.

Serve and enjoy!

Nutritional Information: 268 Cal, 9.9 g Fat, 31 mg Chol, 62 mg Sodium.

Caramel Apple Empanadas

If you want to make a quick dessert then here is the best option for you. This recipe can be prepared within 20 minutes and it is also super delicious.

Ingredients

1 apple, peeled, cut into 8 wedges

1 tbsp lemon juice

1 tbsp granulated sugar

½ tsp ground cinnamon

⅛ tsp ground nutmeg

dash of allspice

½ cup caramel bits

1 tsp milk

1 refrigerated pie crust

1 egg, lightly beaten

sanding sugar to sprinkle on top

Directions

Preheat your oven to 425 F.

Add apples, lemon juice, spices, and sugar to a bowl and mix well. Set aside.

Roll pie crust and cut 8 circles using a cookie cutter.

Line a cookie sheet with parchment paper and place pie crust circles over it.

Melt milk and caramel in a bowl.

Place apple wedges and 1 tsp. caramel mixture on each circle.

Brush the edges of empanadas and seal by using your fingers or a fork.

Now, brush the empanadas with egg wash.

Sprinkle some sugar over empanadas.

Bake for about 15 minutes.

Once done, remove from the oven and serve!

Nutritional Information: 117 Cal, 13 g Fat, 5 mg Chol, 260 mg Sodium, 1.2 g Protein.

Shepherd's Pie Empanadas

Some people like fried empanadas whereas, others like bakes ones. It doesn't matter what your preference is, you can never say no to shepherd's pie empanadas. Here is a quick recipe to make this delicious appetizer:

Ingredients

4 cups of cold leftover Shepherd's Pie

20-30 empanada wrappers

Peanut or lard

Vegetable oil for frying or brushing before baking

Optional:

fresh parlsey for garnishing

Directions

Roll empanada dough and form small rounds using a cookie cutter.

Place 1 tbsp. of mashed potatoes and 1 tbsp. of veggie/meat over the empanada rounds.

Dip your finger in water and rub it around the edges of empanadas.

Fold and seal the empanadas using a fork.

In a deep fryer, heat oil to 350 F.

Fry the empanadas for about 5 minutes.

Once they become golden brown, remove from the fryer and place on a towel lines plate.

Serve and enjoy!

Nutritional Information: 220 Cal, 20 g Fat, 87 mg Chol, 741 mg Sodium.

Chocolate Dulce de Leche Empanadas

Chocolate dulce de leche empanadas are filled with caramel or dulce de leche. Because these empanadas are made with chocolate dough, they are great to satisfy your chocolate cravings.

Ingredients

Chocolate empanada dough

3 cups flour

¾ cup cocoa powder, unsweetened

¼ - ½ cup sugar

Pinch of salt

1 teaspoon cinnamon powder – optional

2 sticks of unsalted butter, cut into small pieces

2 eggs

4-6 tablespoons of water

Dulce de leche filling

2 16 oz jars of dulce de leche

Optional: Dash of salt

1 egg, whisked with 1 tablespoon water (egg wash)

¼ cup demerara sugar

Directions

To make chocolate dough, add all the dry ingredients to a food processor. Mix well.

Add butter and mix again.

Now, add eggs, and 4 tbsp. water to the processor and mix again.

Once done, remove from the processor and transfer to a bowl. Knead well. Divide this chocolate dough into two section and refrigerate for about 30 minutes.

Roll the dough on a floured surface and cut into small rounds.

Place 1 tbsp. dulce de leche on each empanada round and fold them. Seal the empanadas using your finger or a fork.

Brush the empanadas with egg was and sprinkle with demerara sugar.

Preheat your oven at 375 F and bake empanadas for about 20 minutes.

Once done, remove from the oven and sprinkle with cocoa powder.

Serve with a scoop of your favorite ice cream.

Enjoy!

Nutritional Information: 300 Cal, 12 g Fat, 60 mg Chol, 85 mg Sodium, 6 g Protein.

Black Bean Baked Empanadas

If you are a vegetarian or you just want to cook something meatless today, then here is a simple and easy to cook recipe of black bean baked empanadas:

Ingredients

1/4 cup canned sweet corn
1 jalapeno pepper, seeded and diced
1/2 cup black beans, rinsed
1/4 cup salsa
1 tsp cumin

salt & pepper to taste
1/2 lime, juiced
1/4 cup cilantro
14.1oz refrigerated pie pastry
1/2 cup Monterey Jack cheese, shredded

Directions

Mix corn, cilantro, jalapenos, lime juice, black beans, cumin and salsa in a large bowl. Set aside.

Roll pie pastry on countertop and cut rounds using a cookie cutter.

Place one tbsp. of bean mixture over the pastry rounds along with 1 tsp. cheese.

Fold the empanadas and seal using a fork.

Line a baking sheet with parchment paper and place empanadas over it. Bake on 450 F for 10 minutes.

Serve with salsa.

Enjoy!

Nutritional Information: 232 Cal, 13 g Fat, 8 mg Chol, 512 mg Sodium, 6.8 g Protein.

Chicken & Mushroom Baked Empanadas

After reading the instructions and the ingredients, you might think that empanadas are difficult to make but the reality is completely opposite. They are very easy to prepare and you can even save the leftovers to use next time.

Ingredients

For the Dough (Makes 14-16 empanadas):

3¾ cups (18¾ ounces) all-purpose flour

1 tablespoon sugar

1 1/2 teaspoons salt

12 tablespoons (1½ sticks) unsalted butter, cut into cubes and chilled

1¼ cups ice water

1 large egg, beaten

For the filling:

1 pound boneless, diced, skinless chicken breast

6 - 8 ounces mushrooms, diced

1 small onion, chopped

⅓ cup pitted green olives, chopped

⅓ cup golden raisins

1½ teaspoons hot paprika

Few tablespoons olive oil

Splash of wine

salt, to taste

Directions

Add all the dough ingredients to a food processor and process.

Remove the mixture from the processer and knead well.

Divide the dough into two sections and wrap with a plastic sheet. Refrigerate for about one hour

Roll the dough on a floured surface or counter top and cut small rounds using a cookie cutter.

Place one tbsp. of meat mixture over each round.

Fold the edges and seal the empanadas using a fork.

Preheat oven to 435 F. Brush the empanadas with eggs and bake for about 20 minutes.

Serve warm!

Nutritional Information: 278 Cal, 18 g Fat, 102 mg Chol, 356 mg Sodium, 9.3 g Protein.

S'mores Empanadas

These s'mores empanadas are super delicious, buttery, and rich with marshmallow filling. If you are an s'mores lover then you should definitely try this recipe at home.

Ingredients
Dough

2 cups all purpose flour

1/4 teaspoon salt

8 tablespoons cold unsalted butter, cut into pieces

1 egg

3 tablespoons ice cold water

S'mores Empanadas

1 cup of chocolate chips

1 cup mini marshmallows

1 beaten egg

Directions

Place all the dough ingredients in a food processor and process well until the dough forms.

Remove from the processor and refrigerate the dough for about 30 minutes.

Roll the empanada dough on lightly floured counter top and cut small or medium sized rounds using a cookie cutter.

Place chocolate chips along with marshmallows on each round and seal the edges.

Brush the empanadas with eggs.

Bake for about 15 minutes in a preheated oven at 400 F.

Nutritional Information: 216 Cal, 4.7 g Fat, 2.5 mg Chol, 119 mg Sodium, 3 g Protein.

Berry & Ricotta Empanadas

Berry and ricotta empanadas are filled with juicy berries and ricotta. This recipe is different than traditional empanada recipes because it brings a unique and sweet touch to empanadas.

Ingredients

2 1/2 cups all purpose flour

2 tbsp sugar

pinch of salt

1/2 cup diced cold butter

1 egg yolk

iced cold water

1 1/4 cup ricotta cheese

14-16 blackberries

2 tbsp milk to brush the unbaked empanadas

powder sugar to dust (optional)

Directions

Add sugar, butter, flour, egg yolk, iced water and salt to a food processor. Process well until the dough is formed.

Remove the dough from the processor and wrap in a plastic sheet. Refrigerate this dough for 1 hour.

Preheat your oven to 400 F and line a baking sheet with parchment paper.

Roll the empanada dough on the lightly floured surface and cut small or medium-sized rounds using a cookie cutter.

Place 1 tbsp. ricotta cheese on each round. Top this ricotta cheese with a berry.

Seal the empanadas using a fork and brush with milk.

Transfer the empanadas to a baking sheet and bake for about 15 minutes.

Once done, remove from the oven and sprinkle with powdered sugar.

Serve and enjoy!

Nutritional Information: 200 Cal, 14 g Fat, 59 mg Chol, 299 mg Sodium.

Roasted Veggie Empanadas

Are you a veggie-lover? If yes, then we guarantee that you will surely fall in love with these roasted veggie empanadas. You can also freeze the empanadas and use later.

Ingredients

Dough:

4½ cups white whole wheat flour

1 tbsp. kosher salt

1 cup (8 oz.) cold unsalted butter, cut into 1/2-inch cubes

2 large eggs

2/3 cup ice water

2 tbsp. distilled white vinegar

Filling:

2 medium eggplants

Olive oil

Salt and pepper, to taste

16 oz. mushrooms, chopped

1 large onion, chopped

1 red bell pepper, seeded and chopped

2 cloves garlic, minced

1 large egg lightly beaten with 1 tbsp. water, for brushing

Directions

Add all the dough ingredients to a food processor and process until the dough is formed.

Remove from the processor and refrigerate for about 30 minutes.

After 30 minutes, roll the empanada dough on lightly floured counter top and cut into rounds using a cookie cutter.

Preheat oven to 375 F.

Slice the eggplant and place these slices on a baking sheet.

Season the eggplants with salt and pepper and brush with olive oil.

Bake for about 35 minutes while occasionally flipping the slices.

Once done, remove from the oven and let cool. When cool, cop the slices and transfer to a bowl.

Just like eggplants, roast other veggies for about 20 minutes. When cool, mix these veggies with eggplant.

To assemble the empanadas, roll the empanada dough on lightly floured counter top and cut small or medium-sized rounds using a cookie cutter.

Place 1 tbsp. of veggie filling on each empanada round and fold it.

Seal the empanadas using your finger.

Preheat your oven to 400 F and bake the empanadas for about 20 minutes.

Serve with salsa!

Nutritional Information: 188 Cal, 8 g Fat, 5 mg Chol, 400 mg Sodium, 4 g Protein.

Breakfast Empanadas

If you are tired of the boring breakfast, then use this recipe to make delicious breakfast empanadas. These empanadas are rich with protein and they also contain fewer calories as compared to other buttery breads.

Ingredients

8 frozen empanada wrappers, thawed
3 eggs
5 egg whites
1/4 teaspoon salt
1/4 teaspoon black pepper
1/2 red bell pepper, minced
3 scallions, minced
Cooking spray
7 ounces cooked chicken breakfast sausage links, (cut into ¼- inch pieces)
1/2 cup (2 ounces) low-fat Swiss cheese, grated
Egg wash (1 egg whisked with 1 tablespoon water)

Directions

Preheat your oven to 425 F.

Line a baking sheet with parchment paper.

Mix egg whites, pepper, scallions, bell pepper, eggs and salt in a bowl.

Spray a skillet with cooking spray and add eggs to it. Cook for 1 minute and add cheese and sausages.

Roll the empanada wrapper on lightly floured countertop and cut medium sized rounds using a cookie cutter.

Place 2 tbsp. of filling on each empanada round. Fold and seal the empanadas using a fork.

Transfer the empanadas to a baking sheet and brush with egg wash.

Bake for about 15 m minutes or until the empanadas turn golden brown.

Serve and enjoy!

Nutritional Information: 230 Cal, 12 g Fat, 48 mg Chol, 766 mg Sodium, 7 g Protein.

Colombian Empanadas

Colombian empanadas are one of the most popular snacks that people love in Colombia. They are stuffed with ground meat and served with lime wedges.

Ingredients

Vegetable oil for frying

Lime for serving

Dough:

2 cups water

1 tablespoon vegetable oil

½ tablespoon sazon Goya with azafran

1 ½ cups precooked yellow cornmeal

½ teaspoon Salt

Filling:

1 chicken or vegetable bouillon tablet

1 tablespoon olive oil

¼ cup chopped white onions

2 cups peeled and diced white potatoes

1 cup chopped tomato

½ teaspoon salt

¼ cup chopped green onions

1 chopped garlic clove

2 tablespoon chopped fresh cilantro

2 tablespoon chopped red bell pepper

¼ teaspoon black pepper

½ pound ground pork and beef

Directions

Add all the dough ingredients to a bowl and knead for about 5 minutes.

Once done, cover and set aside.

To make the filling, add water, potatoes and bouillon tablet to a pot and cook for 20 minutes. Once done, drain excess water and mash potatoes.

In a skillet, heat 1 tbsp. olive oil and add onion to it. Cook for 5 minutes and then add tomatoes, black pepper, cilantro, garlic, green onions and bell pepper. Cook for another 15 minutes.

Add ground meat to the pot and cook again for about 20 minutes.

Once done, transfer this mixture to a bowl and add mashed potatoes in it.

Roll the empanada dough on lightly floured counter top and cut small or medium-sized rounds using a cookie cutter.

Pace 2 tbsp. of meat filling on each empanada circle and fold properly. Seal the empanadas using your finger or a fork.

Take a large pan and add vegetable oil to it. Heat it to 360 F.

Fry the empanadas for 2 minutes each side.

Once done, transfer the empanadas to a plate.

Serve with lime wedges!

Nutritional Information: 189 Cal, 12 g Fat, 34 mg Chol, 357 mg Sodium.

Strawberry Empanadas

If you want to cook something different that does not contain any meat or veggies, then here is a quick and easy recipe of strawberry empanadas. This recipe is going to be a hit on your dining table.

Ingredients

Dough:

½ tsp salt

3 tsp piloncillo, grated

2 sticks of butter, diced and chilled

3 cups all-purpose flour

¾ milk, chilled and divided

Filling:

1 tsp cinnamon

¼ cup brown sugar

2 cups strawberries, diced

For egg wash:

1 egg beaten with 1 tbsp of milk

Directions

Add all the flour ingredients to a bowl and knead until a smooth dough is formed. Refrigerate for 2 hours.

Heat oven to 400 F.

Roll the empanada dough on the lightly floured surface and cut 4 rounds using a cookie cutter.

To make the filling, add strawberries, brown sugar and cinnamon to a pot and cook on medium heat for 16 minutes.

Once done, let cool and transfer to a bowl.

Place 1 tbsp. strawberry filling on each empanada circle and fold it.

Seal the edges of empanadas using a finger or a fork. Brush with egg wash.

Bake these empanadas in a preheated oven for 15 minutes.

Nutritional Information: 300 Cal, 13 g Fat, 10 mg Chol, 110 mg Sodium, 3 g Protein.

Mushroom & Cheese Empanadas

Making empanadas is very easy especially when you have a delicious and quick recipe with you. Here is a recipe of mushroom and cheese empanadas. It has an incredible taste and your kids will surely love it.

Ingredients

2 tbs butter

2 ½ to 3 cups sliced mushrooms

12-15 medium size empanada discs

2 cups sliced shallots

1-2 tsp balsamic vinegar

1 cup grated fontina cheese

¼ cup raisins

1 egg, white and yolk separated and lightly whisked

Directions

Melt butter in a skillet and add shallots and mushrooms to it. Cook for about 15 minutes.

Add balsamic vinegar along with the raisins to the skillet and cook for another 5 minutes. Remove from the heat.

Place 1 tbsp. of the mushroom filling on each empanada disc along with some grated cheese.

Fold the empanadas and seal by using a fork.

Brush with egg whites and then egg yolks.

Transfer the empanadas to a baking sheet and refrigerate for about 30 minutes.

After 30 minutes, bake in a preheated oven for 20 minutes at 400 F.

Serve warm!

Nutritional Information: 200 Cal, 10 g Fat, 10 mg Chol, 210 mg Sodium.

Raisin & Arroz con Leche Empanadas

Arroz con leche is a delicious dish but it is not easy to eat it while you are going for a picnic. An easy to make alternative is these raisin and Arroz con leche empanadas that you can make and pack in your lunch box easily.

Ingredients

1 cup long-grain white rice

1 large cinnamon stick

1 pinch salt

2 cups water

1 can evaporated milk

1/3 cup California raisins

1 teaspoon vanilla extract

¾ cup condensed milk

½ cup sweetened coconut, shredded

1 egg, beaten

1 9" inch readymade pie dough, thawed

flour for dusting

Directions

Add water, cinnamon stick, salt and rice to a pot and bring it to a boil. Cook for about 10 minutes and then add milks and cook again for 5 minutes.

Add raisins to the pot and cook for another 3 minutes. Remove from the heat.

Preheat your oven to 450 F.

Roll the pie dough on lightly floured counter top and cut 3 rounds.

Place 2 tbsp. rice mixture and 1 tsp. of coconut on each circle.

Fold and press the edges to seal the empanadas.

Place these empanadas on a baking sheet and brush with egg.

Bake for 15-20 minutes.

Serve!

Nutritional Information: 133 Cal, 0.2 g Fat, 0.9 mg Chol, 33 mg Sodium, 3 g Protein.

Argentinian Beef Empanadas

This Argentinian beef empanada gives an exotic twist to your traditional empanada recipes. It is super easy to make and is loved by all.

Ingredients

For the dough:

2 1/4 cups of flour

1 tablespoon of distilled white vinegar
1 stick of cold unsalted butter, diced

1 1/2 teaspoons of salt
1 large egg
1/3 cup of ice water

For the filling:
1 tablespoon of smoked paprika
1/2 red bell pepper, seeded and diced

salt and pepper, to taste

1/2 pound of lean ground beef
1 tablespoon of parsley, chopped finely
1/2 large onion, finely chopped
olive oil
1 hard-boiled egg, roughly chopped

1 tablespoon of capers, finely chopped

1 tablespoon of ground cumin
1 cup of chopped, canned tomatoes

1 egg, gently beaten with a fork (for the egg wash)

Directions

Add all the flour ingredients to a bowl and knead well until there are no lumps in the dough. Refrigerate for 2 hours.

To make the empanada filling, add 1 tbsp. olive oil to a skillet. Add pepper and onions and cook for about 6 minutes.

Add tomatoes to the skillet and cook for another 5 minutes.

Now add the beef along with all the remaining filling ingredients to the skillet.

Cook until the beef is cooked properly.

Preheat oven to 400 F.

Roll the empanada dough on lightly floured counter top and cut small or medium sized rounds using a cookie cutter.

Place 1 tbsp. filling on each empanada circle and fold. Press the edges to seal the empanadas.

Brush the empanadas with egg wash.

Bake for about 25 minutes.

Serve and enjoy!

Nutritional Information: 432 Cal, 9.6 g Fat, 58 mg Chol, 966 mg Sodium.

Also, by the editors at Savour Press's kitchen

The Chili Cookbook

The Quiche Cookbook

Indian Instant Pot Cookbook

The Cajun and Creole Cookbook

The Grill Cookbook

The Burger Book

The Ultimate Appetizers Cookbook

The West African Cookbook

Korean Seoul Cookbook

Conclusion

Thank you so much for downloading this eBook. We at Savour Press hope this book has increased your knowledge regarding some unique empanada recipes. This eBook contains a curated list of what we believe to be the best-empanada recipes which encompass a variety of flavors and tastes and can be made easily. While writing these recipes, we made sure that every ingredient should be easily available and that the recipes should be quick and easy to follow. It does not matter whether you want a full meal, or you want to make some nutritious food for your family, this book has everything that you need. We hope you will enjoy cooking with these recipes.

Thanks again for your support.

Happy Cooking!